GW01220311

THROUGH THE VOID

MY JOURNEY FROM SINGLE TO SOULMATE

A GUIDE TO FINDING THE LOVE OF YOUR LIFE

TAMRA MERLOS

©2021 All rights reserved. No part of this publication may be reproduced, distributed, or transmitted in any form or by any means, including photocopying, recording, or other electronic or mechanical methods, without the prior written permission of the publisher, except in the case of brief quotations embodied in critical reviews and certain other noncommercial uses permitted by copyright law.
ISBN 978-1-38619-907-6

Sometimes all falls apart...
You are deconstructed...
You wake up to your life's purpose.

NOVEMBER 2006

I woke up crying.

I was dreaming. I realized that I had not dreamed in years.

It was as if I had been holding my breath all this time.

I dreamed that I climbed up on top of a space within my bathroom, my fingers searching up high. I was looking for a lost wedding ring. As I climbed, I discovered a hidden window. Looking out, I could see vast horizons to the right and left. I saw beautiful green fields and snow-covered mountains.

AUGUST 2007

HOW IT BEGAN
I was sitting at a table at the Eldorado Resort in Reno, Nevada. I had my feet propped up on a chair, legs extended, and I was reading a book on my passion, trail hiking. I was mapping out all the places I wanted to take the friends who would be meeting me in Tahoe for the weekend.

My eyes glanced over to a table of men in the middle of the restaurant, and there in the group was a face I recognized. It was Mathew McConaughey—or so I thought. I looked and looked, unabashedly, embarrassingly, to see if it was him. It wasn't–his jaw was too strong–but I kept staring. Then, he was staring back at me.

I quickly shifted my eyes back to my book, then looked up a couple more times to communicate, *I am here. Please come talk to me.* I peeked over once more, but he was gone.

Oh. Sigh. I went back to reading, finished my salad, and paid.

I walked around the corner and stopped abruptly when I ran into a very tall man with smiling crinkles around his eyes, looking down at me. He said, "What are you reading?"

I bit my lip so I wouldn't flash a toothy green smile and asked him if he would please excuse me while I ran to the restroom. He did, and as I looked at my reflection in the bathroom mirror, I blinked several times in the realization that the Mathew McConaughey lookalike was just outside the restaurant, waiting to talk to me!

I checked my smile and walked back out to meet him. We smiled and talked for some time. He told me his name and asked for mine. His name was D.

The next day, D. left a package for me at my hotel. A book. I smiled to myself, thinking, "He knows me already." I flew home to Las Vegas, feeling giddy.

D. called almost every day, and we spent hours in deep conversation. I was a pharmaceutical rep with a large territory that led me back and forth between Vegas and Reno, and when I came back into town, he picked me up at my hotel for dinner.

It was our first meeting in person since our encounter at the Eldorado. By this time, there had been so many conversations between us that while I didn't exactly remember what he looked like, I felt like I already knew him already.

I had on skinny jeans, sling-back heels, and a t-shirt when he picked me up. He caught his breath as I approached him, and it felt like once again, I was blinking back unbelief at the chemistry between us. He whispered in my ear that I took his breath away, and I believed him.

He had this way about him that I had not encountered. He would stare intensely into my eyes until I reacted in embarrassment and looked down or away. Then, he would gently turn my face back towards his and look into my eyes again, not letting them stray until I finally settled into his gaze. It had a powerful effect.

In the following weeks, we would talk and meet as often as possible. The last time I left on a plane for Vegas, he walked with me to the security line and stayed with me until I had to leave.

We stood close, soaking in each other's presence. He looked at me again with his intense, serious gaze, and as we parted, my heart was begging for an opportunity to stay. I wanted to be near him.

That week, I made a bold move and I asked my company to relocate me to Reno. To my surprise, they did! My sales force in Las Vegas was going through a change, so if I moved, I would have a new product and territory, this time covering Reno and Sacramento.

It all happened so quickly; I didn't even question the move.

I found a cute condo in northwest Reno that backed up to the Peavine mountain range.

D. encouraged my move and offered to drive me from Vegas to Reno. We spent hours talking about our upbringing, aspirations, and things we loved. He told me I was the most wonderful person he had ever met.

Ditto, I thought.

Time with D. felt like breathing in a life force, and I wasn't ready to exhale.

DECEMBER 2007

I was in a new town, with a new job and a new territory, had bought a new house, and had boxes all around. I went to an ugly sweater Christmas party and was enjoying meeting new friends. I talked with someone that I had met on the plane from Vegas to Reno as I moved from my old job to the new one.

She and I had similar interests, and I listened intently as she told me about her life and the job she loved in Vegas. That conversation stuck with me all night, and as soon as I got home from the party, I went to the internet to find the company she had told me about.

As I scrolled down the page, I found descriptions of some of the services offered and some of the people working there. I couldn't believe my eyes when I saw a picture of my guy, D.!

I smiled to myself and read his profile. He lived in Reno... had a dog... and was married to his wife....

Married? He was *married*?

Everything shifted in an instant. It felt like the whole room around me spun 360 degrees and lifted up several levels.

I was silent, literally silent for longer than I had ever been.

I had no words... only deeper and deeper realizations.

A week passed.

Only quiet.

It snowed that week. I hate the cold.

New job. New town.

Could I go back to Vegas, to my job and friends there? How could I get out of this mess, this pain.

Sometimes you can't go back, I thought. The only way out... would be through.

I cut off all communication with D. after leaving him a message saying that I knew he was married. Unfortunately, we worked half a mile from each other, and I was continually afraid that I would see him. Part of me hoped I would.

I knew that I had to be the master of my mind and control my thoughts, but that seemed impossible with so many daily reminders.

A month would pass and then out of the blue I would get a random text from D.

"Would kill to see you."

"Isn't getting any easier."

"I won't forget you."

I am actually grateful for the messages he sent. Though I couldn't respond or pursue him, it helped me to know that he felt the same anguish I was going through.

A SIGN

JULY 2008

One day after work that following summer, I drove to the mountain to hike.

It would be getting dark soon, so I parked my company car (a white Lexus—bless my boss) close to the trailhead and put on my trail-running shoes.

I put my car key into a small pocket in my running shorts, locked the car, and started to run.

Running up a soft dirt hill under the trees is my idea of heaven. I love the smell of pine, the color of the changing aspen trees, and the gentle climb to the top.

That night, I went fast because of the approaching darkness. I ran a seven-mile loop and returned to my car just as the sun went down.

I searched and searched for my key but it was gone. I had secured it in my shorts pocket, so it must have fallen out along the way. It could be anywhere on the seven miles of trail I'd covered—the trail that was now dark.

Even if it were light outside, I began to worry I might not find it at all. The trail was covered in leaves and dirt and rocks, and the key was so small.

How would I ever find it? My boss would kill me if I didn't.

I called a friend to pick me up and determined to get to the trail early the next morning and somehow find that key.

The next day, I took a cab to the trail and began to walk under the trees, looking along the ground every step of the way.

How would I even see it?

It could be under a branch in the first yard or seven miles back at the edge of the creek or under a rock somewhere in the middle! I searched and searched until I finally began to run, full pace, without looking down. I ran about five miles and then slowed down.

I said to myself, *I feel like I'm walking blind.... I feel like I'm walking blind.... I feel like I'm walking blind!*

I ran another two miles before I decided to turn back, and there, several feet off the path, I saw a glimmer of metal. My key!

I reached down and picked it up, only to fall to my knees in tears.

I was sobbing.

I found it.

I found it.

I looked upward for a long time.

It was so clear now.

If you keep walking blind long enough, you will begin to see with other eyes.

As I walked back to the car, once again, I felt like all had shifted. The earth was elevated beneath my feet. Lessons were pouring into my mind so fast I could barely keep up.

If I can see it, it's out there for me, I said to myself. It would not be D., but now I knew what it would feel like. It would be that connection, or at least the same spirit of it... in another package.

Love like that, in another package.

This time, I had to do something new. I had to release, I had to trust. It would be safer to step into that space, the broad unknown horizon, than to stay put.

I remembered my dream from a few years back.

It was time to believe.

That night and the next day—and for the weeks and months to come—I would set out on a journey with God.

Here are the lessons I learned.

A NEW DAY

I had so many questions.

Why did I make the mistake I had made? Could I even trust my own heart... my own mind... my own gut to lead me?

I had really thought he was "the one."

Why didn't I protect and treasure myself? I had a great life in Vegas, one that I built from scratch several years prior. I had a successful career, great friendships, and hobbies to pursue every weekend.

Why was I so quick to move for a relationship? I'd left my huge place on the golf course, and now I was stuck in the cold with snow all around in a small condo instead.

Could I trust myself at all? I thought back to the weeks prior to moving. A string of events occurred that I completely disregarded. Now they glared with meaning.

I'd run out of gas in a rental car while heading to the airport because the gas gauge was faulty. I stood on the side of the road in the heat, wearing my nice Theory business suit, until

Tamra Merlos

the rental car company came to pick me up. I barely made my flight.

That same week, I'd had a flat tire in a rental car, in the worst part of town, and had to call someone to come change my tire so I could get back to work.

I kept losing my keys, and to top it off, my house in Las Vegas was broken into in broad daylight while I was out. I was robbed—only a week before I moved to Reno. Thieves had broken in through a side window, and it took several days for someone to come repair it.

I had to go to work and sleep knowing my house was vulnerable. At night, I locked my bedroom door and slept with a golf club beside my bed.

Soon, I packed up my things, watched my car and all my belongings drive away in a moving truck, and took my final flight from Vegas to Reno.

I sat on the plane and stared out the window, looking one last time at the Las Vegas strip, palm trees, and pink sunset in the distance. What was ahead?

I felt like I was sprinting with no traction. I had no control. It was as if the whole universe was telling me to *stop*.

But I wasn't listening.

I was too focused on rushing forward. I never considered listening to the signs around me. I was too busy for that.

JANUARY 2008

When the student is ready, the teacher appears.

I was listening now.

I sat on my sofa and looked out the sliding glass door as flurries of snow blew by and piled up on the patio just outside. I sat and sat and listened to the quiet. God had more control than I'd thought.

I began to write:

"I feel like I am being prepared for something—like a journey of my spirit, mind, and soul. The tests are ones of faith against fear. Frightful things and times have come to me. Those things that are not solid, the things I fear, have been shaken and tested.

"All is raw and real and firmly placed—I am ready for growth on the bare ground of my life.

The test is to live day by day with no expectation for the future. This is the way to true living and happiness. The test is fear in every area. To learn to face it, stare it down, and press through it.

"I will need deep reservoirs of strength in the days to come. I will pull from these lessons again and again, and they will keep me safe."

To build my life from scratch again would involve introspection. What did I really want? What brought real happiness based on truth, not based on fear or approval?

I would have to choose what was most important to me. I would commit, execute, and have the self-discipline to follow through on living true to these values.

It would take trust, patience, perseverance. This would not be a quick fix. It would take time.

I would have to trust in the invisible hand of God to bring what I needed and enable me to go through the joy and pain of today.

I wanted a rulebook to follow, but I realized the only rule was *be true to myself*. Anything else was just seeking a guarantee to not fail or be hurt.

It's easier to push someone else than to push yourself to wholeness.

I decided to resign from my job as a pharmaceutical rep and seek a position with a local medical equipment company in Reno. All my drive to move up the corporate ladder with my previous company was gone.

I needed roots. I had to prune and grow. How could I ever settle if I was traveling, spending all my time in a hotel room, in a car, or on a plane? My old company offered me a better position, a 17% pay increase, and double commissions to stay. But I had already moved on internally.

Sometimes, you can't go back. You must choose anew.

I asked around among colleagues for a good medical equipment company that was local.

I got a few names and numbers and went back to the snow-covered hideaway that I now called home. I was supposed to go back to work at my old job on Monday with the new terms, territory and pay increase, but my heart wasn't in it.

In the past, I had spent weeks or even months looking for the perfect job, perfecting my resume, and negotiating for the perfect location. This time, I would try something different. Given my internal state, it was inevitable that I'd try something new. All was surrendered. All could be given or taken away, so why put so much stress on myself?

One company kept coming to mind, so that Friday morning I found the address, drove to the office, and hand-delivered my resume to the receptionist.

I was Zen. In the past, I would have asked for the hiring manager's name and information. I would have immediately followed up with a phone call and email outlining my experience and my desire to work for the company.

This time, I got in my car, drove back home soberly, and sat down on my couch to partake in my now favorite pastime—watching the snow flurries pile up on my patio.

I had just settled in when I received a call from the hiring manager at the medical equipment company where I had just dropped my resume.

He asked if I could please come back in. I said yes!

The manager and owner sat down with me to chat about my resume. I noticed that they kept smiling to each other, and at one point they whispered, "She's the one."

I learned that the job I had applied for had been open for almost 2 years and that they had searched and searched for the right person. They had been about to close the position and go in a different direction. Then I waltzed in that Friday morning and dropped my resume.

I was just what they had been looking for—an experienced pharmaceutical rep who could navigate a flat territory and was gutsy enough to do it alone, with little help and fewer leads.

That was me. I knew about starting from scratch. We needed each other. I negotiated my salary terms and was hired on the spot.

Through the Void

I walked out of the meeting to find my new company car. It was a white Lexus, with heated seats—now I would be warm. I giggled to myself and looked up into the grey sky.

I know where I stand.
I know where my feet climb.
Past fields of pain and mountains of quiet...
Through the dark void and into deep waters...
I find myself.
Resting.
In the palm of His hand.

My new job took me through snow-covered mountains to offices in Reno, Carson City, Carson Valley, Gardnerville, Truckee, and Lake Tahoe. The lonely stretches of highway were long, and sometimes I could see only mountains for miles. For me, driving through that stunning beauty each day felt like going home.

I thought about how we are all born into the world alone—completely alone. We also die alone—there is no one with us at the end. I wanted to stay connected to that knowledge, that understanding. To be okay with that and embrace it as the truest reality—this would be the goal of my life. All else is passing. We are each passing through on our journey home.

I prayed that I would never again lose myself.

For years, I had been on top of the world. Everything was easy, and magic was in my hand. I went fast, rarely stopping to breathe. Ambition had blinded me to the hurts of other people. I was always rushing.

Then all at once, I felt like I was running on pavement that was crumbling. I couldn't get my footing. Nothing worked where everything had always worked before.

All could be taken away in a second.

I had been so sure of myself, and at times unfeeling of others less fortunate than I. Now, I felt the pain of loss for the first time. I promised myself that I would never cause pain for another human being, if possible.

When I talked to people in the offices I visited, I saw them differently. The stories of their lives were more important than the product I had to sell. I felt permeable to their pain.

I thought back to the dream I'd had several years back... and realized that I had not dreamed in years. I didn't have time.

I was holding my breath, trying to manage too many things. All depended on me, I thought. If I let go of anything, things would fall apart.

Now I realized, If I had let go... I could have gotten to my destination sooner.

The river of life had been flowing, and I had been struggling--- holding on to the nearest branch or rock, trying to get to where I thought I should be.

But the river isn't about resistance.

It's about flow.

I really could trust life to lead me.

When you surrender and let go, life will lead you exactly where you want to go.

THEN CAME SPRING

2008

I had made some friends, three that I knew would be lifelong. After work each day, we would meet up and play indoor sports at the nearest community center or take long hikes together. Several times a week, we would run around downtown Reno in short skirts and boots in the cold looking for live music to dance to.

I was determined to devote my time to my friends and to the things that I wanted to do instead of dating. Each time I was asked out, I compared the person to D. Since no one measured up, I said no thanks. I had a few friends who thought I was crazy, that I should be "getting out there." Their concern made me question myself.

Was I setting myself up to be single forever?

A couple of times, I gave into that mentality and went to a political fundraiser or wine tasting that I had been invited to. I felt so out of place. I liked to dress up and go out, but I would much prefer to dance at an outdoor concert than to be indoors, hoping to get noticed by a guy in a suit.

It was not my scene at all. I will never forget the awful feeling of dressing up and going somewhere I didn't want to go, then leaving alone. Those outings were a waste of time I could have enjoyed doing what I wanted to do.

Never again, I told myself. I made a commitment to live the life I wanted all the time. I would not go searching for love or put myself "out there" to be taken.

I started making a list of the people, places, and groups that made me feel icky. The "Bad Vibe" list, I called it.

I then made a list of "Good Vibe" places and people. This included music festivals, biking down the Truckee River, my volleyball league, dancing with friends on the weekend, and hiking almost anywhere.

I hiked 50 miles a week that spring and summer.

I grew up in Texas, where the heat is horrible, the rain pours, the pollen is choking, winters are cold, and fall is fleeting. Now in Reno and Tahoe, I finished each workday with the excitement of going to the trail.

My hikes were a conversation with myself. I was giving my best to life and to all the things that I loved, but I still carried the pain of D.

I had been happy being single for a long time, but I really needed to know that love was out there for me.

I asked for more signs.

Weeks passed.

I voiced my heart upward. "You must show me."

I got into the habit of using yellow sticky notes. Just when I thought I could not make it one more day... I would put an end date on a sticky note and put it on the mirror in my bathroom.

I would make a deal with God. "I will not think on or worry about finding 'the one' until this date. You must show me a sign by this date to get me through this void. After that day, I will allow myself to have a meltdown. Until then, I am trusting you to give a me a sign."

Each time I did this, inevitably, something would happen to "get me through," and I could tear down the little yellow sticky.

This became my practice to get through the pain of uncertainty to the other side— where God was. Signs, miracles, serendipitous events. *Just on the other side*, I would tell myself.

This was just the kind of journey that I had signed up for.

JULY 2009

A SHIFT

My work often required me to attend local fundraisers and community. One Friday night, I got dressed up to attend an annual gala for a local hospital. I met several interesting people, including one of the guest speakers, Henry Winkler.

I kept thinking to myself, "I am ready to meet someone!" Unfortunately, the attendees were CEOs and physicians, most of whom had wives on their arms. I had gotten used to coming and going home alone, but as the evening ended, I left disappointed that this time was no different. I began to drive home.

I had barely eaten at the gala, so I stopped at a gas station close to my house and ran in to get a protein bar before going home. All eyes turned to me as I walked into the store wearing a slinky low-backed dress with strappy high heels. I bought my bar, walked out to my car, and settled into my seat to for my evening meal.

What a waste, I thought. *I feel really beautiful tonight, and once again, I am going home alone.*

I don't want to be alone anymore.

As I started driving, I started crying. "I don't believe in you anymore! I've tried—and it has been so, so long. I have held true, have not dated much because there is no one I am interested in!

"Where are you? Where is my husband? I want my husband!" I shouted.

"If you do not show me a sign, a strong sign, by the morning, this is it. I will stop believing."

I sobbed as I got under the covers that night, not knowing what the morning would bring. I had not talked to God like that before, and I was a little afraid.

The next morning, I rushed into my work clothes and drove to the office. Another day. When a coworker stopped me as I walked in the front door, I had forgotten my anger and words to God from the night before. We didn't talk often. She was in billing, working inside the office, and I was in marketing/sales—always in the field.

I had not spoken a word to her that morning when she approached me, caught my sleeve and said, "He will find you. A man finds a good wife. You don't have to worry about searching. He will find you. The Lord told me to tell you that." And off she went to her desk.

What?! How did she know?

I didn't even really know her. We didn't have mutual friends. I was stunned. Tears streamed from my eyes and onto the elevated ground beneath me.

He came through for me. He showed up…. There was no denying it.

I had needed a sign, and now I felt there were angels all around. Wow.

I sang at the top of my lungs to the heavens. *I beeelieeeve, I beeelieeeeve.*

If I stayed in this state, anything was possible. He could manifest before my eyes right then.

I could see him clearly.... *he was in this town.*

When my soul is ready, he will be there.

JULY 17, 2009

I knew the spark would be instantaneous, the kind you feel when you are going through life with your head down and then stumble on the toes of some beautiful stranger.

Electric.

The connection would have to cut through—spirit to spirit. There would have to be crazy chemistry from the very beginning, or else I didn't want it.

It happened just like that.

It was a summer of music festivals. I travelled to Wanderlust, High Sierra Music Fest, Burning Man, Outside Lands, and all the local fests of Reno and Lake Tahoe. I was finding my own groove and enjoying it.

One warm Friday night, I slipped into my favorite skinny jeans and a low-backed peach shirt— my go-to "feeling sexy" outfit—and went out to meet friends. I parked my car and clipped down the street to meet them. They were late. I wandered around for a while and then sat down at an outdoor café and ordered a drink.

An hour passed and my friends still hadn't arrived. I shook my head in disbelief. I felt stupid now, being stood up by a group of single girls. I took a final sip of my drink and stood to leave. As I did, the performing guitarist caught my attention and motioned for me to stay.

I looked around the room. *Was he talking to me?* My mood started to lift.

Within a few moments, he was standing in front of me and scooping my hands into his. "Where are we going?" I asked.

"I just got off work," he said. "Let's go explore!"

I clasped his warm hand as he led me out of the restaurant and towards a Burning Man exhibit nearby. I glanced back and wondered out loud if I should let my friends know where I was headed. He just smiled and kept walking until we were standing in front of the fire.

I was smiling, too.

It was dark outside and slightly chilly, and he held me close. Light danced around our faces as we held them to the fire and then turned back to each other in conversation.

He was a professional musician, kind, playful, incredibly handsome, and bold. I looked into his dark, Zen eyes and felt a spark I had not felt since D.

Same spirit, different package.

He spoke in the same metaphorical way that I did and with such encouragement that I immediately felt better.

I asked, "You are a spiritual man, aren't you?"

"Ha! That's all I am. Spirit," he said.

I will never forget the words he spoke to me that night. We spent hours running around downtown, sharing our life stories. We ended up along the edge of the Riverwalk.

He pressed against me and whispered, "You are about to have everything you want in life."

I'm not implying that I knew he was "the one" in the moment we met. But I had practiced listening to signs, messages, and intuition, and my practice had made me sharp. I could trust my own heart. I was listening.

Tamra Merlos

I didn't expect to end up loving him so quickly or so deeply. Milton would become my greatest teacher, lover, friend, a true husband, and the father of our beautiful daughter.

 I've heard it said that your soulmate will be someone who teaches you for a lifetime.

I remembered the lessons: the river, the flow.

Don't resist your life. It will lead you exactly where you want to go.

FROM SINGLE TO SOULMATE: A GUIDE TO FINDING THE LOVE OF YOUR LIFE

I knew these lessons weren't just for me. They were gifts to share. There are no shortcuts to wholeness. You have to do the work. If you are not solid, all will fall apart.

I went the long way through the void and woke up to my life's purpose.

GET CLEAR

If you want to manifest the love of your life, first, you must get clear about what you want.

Make a list about your perfect mate and the type of relationship you want.

Mine looked something like this:

- Leader
- Self-motivated
- Has hobbies and friends
- Plays acoustic guitar

- Loves to dance
- Great body
- Not too hairy
- Outgoing
- Spiritually minded

I wanted to be in a monogamous, committed relationship with great intimacy. I wanted to be married.

I am always amazed when I look back to my list, made in January 2008—a year and a half before I met Milton. He is literally everything on my list, down to the guitar and hair!

If you want a life partner and a true soulmate, I challenge you to make your list and stay clear on what you want, Don't be so concerned with the "package" love comes in—you will love the one for you—but definitely include things that are really important for you on your list, down to the smallest detail.

Just think, if you are so great... then why would you marry a slug?

The person for you may have opposite strengths/weaknesses from you, and that is okay! They may be there to encourage you and to be encouraged by you in areas of weakness. This is where wisdom and openness play a part when you encounter someone for the first time. You could miss the one for you if you are too focused on their job or finances, or even their appearance. Those things can change.

Focus on the inside, on how they treat themselves and other people. Where do they want to go in life? Most importantly, do they bring out your best self? Do you bring out theirs?

The one for you will make you want to be a better person. They will need the gifts you have to offer and vice versa. Instead of thinking about what they can give you or what they have to offer, think more about how you can give.

Create your list with some openness for a person's potential.

When I met my husband, he was not making as much money as he wanted, but he was super smart, a hard worker, and had amazing business skills. In a short time, he was flourishing and doing very well. I knew the amazing qualities he had would make him very successful. I was right!

This is a great example of making your list but also being open-minded to areas that can easily change with time.

Characteristics are attitudes and habits that are developed over time and are difficult to change. These can be deal-breakers. I would not recommend getting into any relationship in which there are deal-breakers from the very beginning. For instance, if someone is very lazy in one area of life, they will more than likely display this characteristic in many areas, including the relationship.

Tamra Merlos

If their personal habits are not compatible with yours from the very beginning, do not expect those to change. Use your wisdom on this.

PERFECT MATE

List the qualities of your perfect mate.

1.

2.

3.

4.

5.

YOU GET WHO YOU ARE (OR WHAT YOU BELIEVE YOU DESERVE)

At the end of the day, only you know what is on the inside—who you really are. Like attracts like. You get who you are.

What are your values? Where do you spend your time, money, effort?

If you want a relationship that's full of passion and intimacy, express your passion with your partner. If you want someone faithful, don't cheat! If you're looking for a real commitment, don't date married folks!

Your beliefs and your actions must be congruent, or you are just fooling yourself about who you truly are. So many people want a quality mate, but they are not willing to stop playing, flirting, and being inappropriate with others when they think no one is looking.

If you want something great, be great.

If you are continually attracting losers, people unlike yourself but who you find yourself "in love" with, it could be that you are attracting what you believe you deserve. Low self-esteem or desperation can cause you to accept behaviors in others you would never allow in yourself. Go back to your "getting clear" list and put a strong boundary around yourself. Only allow those into your life that line up with your list. If you have feelings for someone who is not worthy of you, remember to love yourself more.

People learn how to treat you by what you accept. They measure up to your expectations, or they are out.

LIST YOUR VALUES

1.

2.

3.

4.

5.

WHERE DO YOU SPEND YOUR TIME, EFFORT, MONEY?

1.

2.

3.

4.

5.

Your list of values and your list of where you spend time and effort need to measure up. Otherwise, what you say you value is just fantasy based on self-deception. If you spend your time in front of the TV eating cookies and do not exercise, then you do not value your health.

If you say that you value your friends but do not invest any time or money enjoying them, then your values and actions are not congruent.

Whatever you treasure and value, you will spend your effort, time, and money on.

Identify the gaps! Where are your two lists incongruent? These are areas of growth for you.

Ask yourself at the end of every day if you have lived the life you say you want.

If you value your family, spend time with them. If you value your health, exercise and eat a healthy diet. Your habits are where your strengths or weaknesses come to light.

BE THE PERSON YOU WANT

To fully receive love, we must feel worthy of it. You cannot give what you do not have.

You gotta love your life first!

Instead of spending time "dating," do what you love. Your mate will find you there!

After I was single for some time, I asked myself what would happen if I took some time off from "dating" and did what I wanted. What if I just invested in me? Treasured me?

So, I did.

I played in a volleyball league, hiked, biked, travelled to different cities, went to music festivals, and invested in friendships. I took dance classes and self-improvement workshops, volunteered at a local school, worked on my career, read tons of books, and found new music. I truly invested in *me*.

So many people spend time, money, and their efforts on things that do not sustain them. At the end of the day, all you have is your mind, your health, your peace, your experience. The biggest mistake is thinking you have to spend all your time trying to find love. Find yourself!

You are truly your greatest love.

Treasure yourself.

Invest in yourself.

Go to a concert, take a class, travel, read, write, volunteer, join a group.

To share a life, you gotta get a life!

Tamra Merlos

LIST THE HOBBIES, ACTIVITIES, AND THINGS YOU LOVE. DO THEM!

1.

2.

3.

4.

5.

RELEASE WHAT YOU DO NOT WANT

What do you accept in life? It may be the cute-but-not-right-for-you person you keep hanging out with because they are safe, or you are lonely, or they stroke your ego.

You only have space for one love of your life. That space has to remain open for what you truly want. To receive the mate you want, keep your hands free of what you do not want.

Release anything that doesn't measure up to your values. They measure up, or they are out. Period.

I made a list of all the "bad vibe" places and people that I wanted to stay away from…. and I stayed away. That list included some single girlfriends that made me feel like I had to get out there every weekend and look for a man. That list included a couple of nightclubs that made me feel "icky" and a party-hard crowd that left me feeling horrible in the morning and prevented me from being my best self. It included the trickle of men passing through my life who were nice or cute but not marriage material.

If you want that crazy-chemistry, love-their-skin-and-every-thing-inside-them-forever kind of love…you have to be available for love. Otherwise, when the one shows up, you will miss them.

Release past loves that did not work. If it didn't work then, it will not work now. Any thoughts you spend on these people are sheer fantasy. Toughen up.

Be the master of your mind. You alone control what comes into your mind and what you let yourself entertain.

In times of loneliness, stay open and hopeful. When you visualize the new person that is coming for you, do not insert the face or experience of a past love. Leave it open.

Make a list of all the places and people that bring your faith down and then release them.

Here are some great examples of things to release:

Married people, booty call relationships, going out with people you feel no romantic connection with, spending all of your time with couples because you don't want to be alone, going out with people you would not marry.

You can waste lots of time, but if you truly want deep, rich, intimate, crazy-chemistry type of love, you should treasure this resource. Life is not a dress rehearsal!

Release all fantasy loves. Ask yourself if you really want someone halfway across the world, someone unattainable, married, or with a girlfriend. Or do you want real, stunning, new, passionate love for a lifetime with someone who wants you, too?

I know from my own experience that this is very difficult, but you can do it.

I met a wonderful person from Montana at a summer music festival. He made one of the most romantic gestures towards me and won me right away. He drove 12 hours in an unair-conditioned car just to see me over the weekend before returning to work the following Monday morning.

We hiked and went to dinner before he returned home. As he was driving back, he stopped and sent me a copy of a book we had discussed over the weekend. It was wrapped in brown paper with string and mailed from a post office along his 12-hour drive home. He had many qualities I was looking for, and he seemed to care for me—a lot. There was only one problem.

I hate the cold. I would never want to live in Montana, and he had too many roots put down there to consider living somewhere else.

I had to release him.

Very soon after, I met my future husband, Milton, in downtown Reno. Milton knew how I felt about the cold. After dating for two years, getting married, and having a baby, he found a way to move our family to where we now spend our winters, in Southern California.

I smile just thinking about it. You can always trust life to bring you what you want.

Looking back, it seems so hard to believe that I could have ended up chasing love to a place I didn't want to go.

Instead, love found me right where I lived and moved me somewhere warm.

Make sure your needs and desires are not muddy. Everything must be clear. The quicker you release what you don't want, the quicker you can be open and free for what you do want.

Bring closure to any entanglements. Make calls, texts, emails, whatever you need to do to bring closure to the relationships that you do not want.

LIST OF RELATIONSHIPS TO RELEASE

1.

2.

3.

4.

5.

HOW TO RELEASE A PAST LOVE
You must open your hand to love.

Make the decision that it is safer to trust in the unknown with all its possibilities than to hold on to the past.

There is an abundance of love in the world and many opportunities for you to experience something completely new. Only *one thing* can keep you from it.

Imagine a little boy who is holding a fist full of pennies while trying to grasp a dollar bill that is crumpled at the bottom of his pocket. If he lets go of the coins, he can surely pull the bill from his pocket. But like so many of us, he is reluctant to let go of what is in his hand.

If you truly are ready for more, you need to release all that you have been holding. Make a firm list of all the past loves that have been occupying your time and mind and let them go.

For a while, these relationships may have worked for you, but, like the pennies, you need to open your hand and release them for something new.

SWITCH THE CHANNEL
So, what is next after you decide to let go of a past love?

You cannot stop the flow of thoughts and emotions that come after a breakup.

Releasing a past love is difficult enough, but it is the continual state of release that is almost impossible to maintain. When thoughts and memories of your past love fill your mind, you might cry uncontrollably, fall into depression, or start scheming on how to get that person back. Right?

If you let this go on too long, you may find yourself calling or texting that person or falling into destructive patterns. You may feel helpless in the wake of emotion. Know that there is a solution that works.

You can switch the channel.

Imagine yourself sitting on the couch watching television when a horrifying show starts to air. Initially, you feel lazy and allow the show to run. You reach a point where the discomfort of the images pushes you into motion, and you decide to reach for the clicker. You don't rage against the TV or allow the images to pollute your mind. You simply change the channel.

Emotions are like that. Your thoughts are a constant stream of internal images that bring up powerful emotions. Think on them too long, and you are certain to give in to them.

You alone are the master of your mind. Learn to switch the channel by thinking of scenarios that uplift and empower you.

Each time painful thoughts come, you can either indulge them and reap painful consequences, or you can think on something else.

It takes work, but this is the way to escape cyclical, detrimental thoughts.

When I first started this process, it felt there was no gap in time between my painful emotions and the thoughts that created them. After some practice—and many crying episodes—I learned that I did not have to resist the thoughts. All I had to do was to think of something else.

No warfare. No internal battles for my mind.

"Anything but" was my motto.

"Anything but" meant I would switch the channel by turning my attention to things that were interesting or fun. Things that I wanted to think on.

"Anything but" the person I was releasing.

I took care of myself. Splurged on myself. This meant being a little extravagant with myself in the beginning, but in the end, it was worth it to get out of pain.

At times I would catch myself in tears because I was reliving the past. I would immediately put on a favorite CD, call a trusted friend, get an ice-cream cone, or go shopping. I kept audiobooks on hand and would start listening when my mind headed for trouble. Sometimes I threw myself into a project. When the pain was really bad, I knew the best way out—a long hike and a massage.

The worst thing you can do is to stay stuck, watching the horror show in your head.

Switch the channel.

Get prepared before you are in an emotional tailspin. Get some great books, inspirational music, and a list of gym classes that you want to attend. Find local walking trails close by. Have friends to call. List all these resources while you are feeling good, before the pain comes. Make sure you have your go-to list close by at all times so that you are never left unprepared.

I promise, this works.

Do something fun. Do something you love. Over time, your thoughts will stop assaulting you. You will develop great mental and emotional strength. You will step into your power.

PREPARE THE WAY
Whatever you want to bring into your life, you first need to prepare the way. Make a place for what you want.

I had been dating Milton for almost two years. I felt internally married, but I wanted the whole thing… the proposal, the ring, the wedding on the beach. I wanted to be married to Milton.

I wondered where his heart and mind were, and then I thought, "Instead of focusing on him, what would happen if I decided to focus on me?"

What was my part? Was I ready?

If he asked me to marry him tomorrow, could I say "yes"?

I needed to prepare the way.

So many people want to get married but they have unknown blocks that prevent or prolong the wait. I have heard of people trying to date and move on before they are officially divorced, or while they are still living in the same house with a past mate or love. This never works.

I sat down and made a list of all the things I needed to clear up before I could truly be ready.

There were old pictures of past loves still in photo albums in my closet. My Facebook page needed a tune up, and I needed to go through my junk-filled garage.

It was tedious. I spent several weekends at home and many nights after work taking care of my list.

When I lifted the last load into the dumpster and crossed the last to-do off my list, Milton asked me to marry him.

It was like a dream. Milton does nothing halfway, and his proposal was no exception. He asked me to pack a bag one

Friday afternoon and whisked me off to go hike the Flume trail overlooking Lake Tahoe. When we reached the top, he got down on one knee and proposed, ring in hand.

I sank down in the sand beside him and looked at him a long time before saying yes. I loved him so much.

Life had brought us together with so much magic. It was a moment I would never forget. It took me a while to embrace it all and finally speak.

He looked at me expectantly and asked again. This time I caught up to the emotion of it all. "Yes...yes!" I said. Then I looked at my hand, the ring. It was stunning. I would have accepted a thread around my finger.

He then led me down the mountain, and we met up with our friends at a private six-bedroom place overlooking the lake. Wow.

I can never convey the joy of the moment knowing my life was clear—garage and all—and I could just say "yes!"

We got married just a few months later, on the beach, at sunset, with family all around. It was worth it to be ready.

I have also seen people who want to move on from a past love and start dating someone seriously, but they are unwilling to clean up their Facebook accounts. They then wonder why the relationship doesn't move as quickly as they wanted or is filled with distrust.

Do unto others as you would have them do to you. Do you really want to be dating someone, falling in love with them, then to find love notes or old photos of past loves lying around?

You get what you give. Make it your mission to make the person you love feel like they are the only person on the planet. Let them know they are special. They will treat you the same.

Make your list of things to clean up to prepare your way. This may be finances, debt, legal matters, old love letters or pictures, social media accounts, and so on. The sooner you clean these up, the sooner you can be fully ready for your true love!

LIST THE ACTIONS YOU NEED TO TAKE TO BE READY:

1.

2.

3.

4.

5.

MASCULINE AND FEMININE ENERGY

Growing up, young boys do not look into their future and think, *Someday I want to marry an independent girl. She will not need me much, and for this I will love her.*

I have to smile at that idea.

No, like it or not, men would probably tell you something like this.

Someday, I am going to find a beautiful girl who loves and needs me, and she will think I am smart and wise and listen to me and depend upon me. I will swoop that girl up and marry her and I will never let her fall.

That is the voice of the masculine.

As men in today's world, that romantic voice of the masculine rarely gets to be heard.

Women today have grown accustomed to using their own masculine energy to pursue education and careers and to excel alongside men. They need that side to accomplish goals and take care of themselves. This is good–in work.

Not so much in love.

Women still have the feminine inside, the receptive, the open, the emotional, the vulnerable…. but they have been misled. Women are taught that they must be tough, bold, assertive, and even aggressive to win. This is true, at work or outside the relationship.

Not in love.

The masculine will always look for a polar opposite to join.

The giver and the receiver. The lover and the beloved.

Women should know that they can be as tough as nails all day long in their world, but when they come home to their lover… they can be soft.

This is what men dream of as little boys. All their hardness softens when it is received.

It's the embrace at the end of the day. Its beauty and grace against the brashness of the world. It's the thing that a man loves and treasures and works all his life for—the beautiful woman that receives him.

Women need masculine men too!

The mindset of the masculine is to always treasure, protect, and provide. Never to leave.

A man who is truly the leader of his household will always bring great security to his wife, kids, and family.

The role of the dad is to be a strong leader. If the family has a problem, we run to Dad to fix it. If the wife is on overload due to all she has to do with work and the kids, she knows whom to run to. She has the deep security that everything will be okay because her husband is a strong man and he can handle it. When problems come, it's his powerful arms that hold all together. He is not the kind that runs away and hides when trouble comes.

It's the power of his love that says, "I'll take care of you. I will never leave. I'll hug you closer."

FEMININE ENERGY IS:
Receptive
Nonverbal
Peaceful
Flowing
Open
Allowing
Listening
Following
Supportive

WOMEN—HOW TO DEVELOP YOUR FEMININE ENERGY
Okay, ladies. You do not need to be a doormat, let a guy call all the shots, or pretend to be something you are not.

Remember, we all have both masculine and feminine parts of our personality. You need them both!

The next few paragraphs are designed for those independent women who don't need a man to be happy but want one. If you are a high-powered woman who finds it difficult to receive, this guide will help you to *develop* your feminine side. These practices will magnetize the masculine. It may go against your instincts at first to tap into your feminine energy. As you practice, though, you will notice how men are attracted to you.

Be receptive.

Look at your man in the eyes and fully listen when he is sharing.

Use quiet to fill the space between you.

If he has a plan to take you somewhere or do something.... *let him* lead without offering your opinion or changing the plan.

Allow him to take charge.

Allow him to lead, even when you think you can do it better.

If he offers to help you lift something or open a door, say thank you so much and *accept* the help. Of course you can accomplish these tasks on your own, but when you just accept, flow, and receive without blocking, you are allowing him to be masculine.

Do you really want to carry the load all the time?

Men are often shy of planning or leading because they get so much resistance.

Think about how wonderful it feels to have an idea or plan and then share it with someone who just says "okay, great, let's do it!" You are encouraged to do more when you get positive feedback.

When you change your man's plan, offer advice, or criticize him, what he hears is "rejection." "Why try?" he thinks to himself. "She won't like it anyway, so I just won't try."

The more you can just say yes, the more he will feel encouraged to plan, be creative, romantic, pursuing, and leading. As he is more confident, he will look for ways to please you. He will come to understand what you like because he gets such positive reinforcement when he tries! Eventually, he will lead without you having to prompt him.

You help your man become the leader of your relationship, home, and family when you allow him to lead. Men naturally love this. It is also extremely rewarding to follow. Whoever takes the lead takes the hit if you fall.

It is very wearying to always be in control, take charge, entertain, and pursue. It is so freeing to flow, allow, follow. This is especially true once you have children and you are the full-time CEO of their world. There are some things only a mother can do for her children. While a mother handles these responsibilities, she will need and want the support of a mate.

If a man feels like he is responsible for you and your family, he will protect and provide. He will take great pride in it. This is the kind of strength you want for yourself and your children.

It is shortsighted not to let our men plan a date without criticism or resistance. We must think long-term. Think about how wonderful it must feel when he has been working in a masculine world and then comes home to your feminine warmth.

Be his home.

Let him call you first. *Let* him pursue you. *Let* him do the work of coming up with a date, a plan, and then *accept* it, even if you may want to offer other suggestions. Just go.

If he offers you something, say yes. If you have a "better" idea, keep it to yourself.

You are choosing to hold back on saying all that you know. This challenges the masculine within you and allows you to develop your feminine side.

Look individuals in the eye if they are talking. Do not interrupt. When someone is telling a story, *refrain* from telling your story or piggybacking on theirs with your own additions.

Just *accept*. Listen fully without blocking. You will be amazed at how difficult this is if you have a lot of masculine energy. You will naturally want to "tell," to give advice and assert your opinions.

These are all masculine attributes. If these are strengths for you, then you might be bringing them to your relationship. Practice using your feminine side with your man and notice the wonderful way he reacts to you.

MASCULINE ENERGY IS:
Forceful
Aggressive
Assertive
Leading
Phallic
Telling
Critical
Providing
Pursuing

MEN—HOW TO DEVELOP YOUR MASCULINE ENERGY
Okay, guys. Here is a cheat sheet on attracting a true feminine goddess.

Be strong.

Take the lead.

Treasure and protect what you love.

Call instead of text.

Make the first move.

Pursue what you want.

Make a plan.

Write down your goals.

When you invite someone out on a date, have a plan and pay.

If your resources are limited, invite them to do something that is fun and free.

Women love walking and talking, smelling the roses, going to the library, taking hikes, getting foot massages, and going to museums or sporting events. Find out what she really enoys.

The worst thing you can do is to show up at your date's house and ask, "So, what should we do?"

Keep your attention on your date/mate while you are with them. Not doing this can kill the strongest attraction and affection between you two. Women want to feel special and protected. If you are looking at or noticing other women, you will make your date/mate feel threatened.

Women naturally protect themselves. If they feel threatened or unloved, they will shut down and emotionally run away from you because you are dangerous to them.

They will wonder about your intentions if you do not focus your eyes and attention fully on them.

If you are dangerous, you are not protector/provider, husband, and father-of-their-children material. Got it? Good.

Clean up your Facebook or social media accounts as soon as you are sure you are pursuing "the one" for you. Women will run if they sense you are a player. Date one woman at a time.

If a relationship doesn't work, release it fully and move on cleanly. No lingering texts or late-night calls, please. Stay clear for your one.

Pay their way on dates. Of course they can pay, but you are showing them how you are going to be in the relationship.

Protector, provider, pursuer. That is you.

Every person has both masculine and feminine parts of their personality. Every day, we use these parts in varying degrees to reach our goals and maintain healthy, vibrant relationships.

The truly balanced partnership will allow each individual to use both their masculine and feminine energy within the relationship. This is give and take, and it is the passion that glues us together.

Someone must talk while the other listens. One must lead the way while the other follows.

This is never one-sided; both take turns and flow smoothly from leader to follower, giver to receiver, lover to beloved.

True passion and chemistry between a couple is achieved when the masculine pursues and the feminine receives. Sometimes, it is the female companion that takes the lead. She plans a trip, tells her lover what to bring, when to show up, and what to wear. She is happy to use her masculine energy, and he is happy to let her do so. He can relax and enjoy the ride.

Sometimes it is the male who wraps his arms around his lover, lifts her onto the couch and cuddles her in close for an unexpected warm kiss. She is happy to relax back into his strong grip and receive him.

These are examples of each partner using the different energies within themselves and within the relationship. The most passionate couples are great givers and receivers, and they know when to give and take.

KEYS TO A LONG-TERM LOVE RELATIONSHIP

List a few things you need in life to be happy. This is your "must" list.

For example, I couldn't care less about going to movies or dining out. The "musts" for me are healthy food, long hikes, walks, or bike rides, and occasionally dressing up—really up—and going out to an extravagant meal, a fancy hotel, or dancing.

I like to mix things up every now and then and want to feel sexy, pretty, and alive in the world.

That's it! Being outdoors, church, and time with friends and family complete my life most of the time and don't leave me fearing what I might be missing.

Social media outlets and other entertainment outlets are big "time wasters" for me. When I am forced to learn the latest technology, I am just itching to get back to my real loves, the outdoors or my beloved books. It is who I am.

So, what is it for you? What makes you tick?

Make a list of the "musts" in your life and be committed to maintaining them once you are in your perfect relationship.

So many people drop everything they love to do when they enter a new relationship. They then wonder why, after a few months or years, they feel depressed or resentful towards the partner who is "keeping them" from their life.

You alone are responsible for your happiness.

It takes effort to organize your time and relationship with your own needs in mind, *but that is what being happy in a relationship requires.*

Your partner doesn't make you happy. You do.

When you put yourself first, it doesn't mean that you only please yourself. A relationship is about giving, helping, and sharing life together. Sometimes, that means you won't get to do what you want to do. But you need to maintain the "musts" in your life.

You may fear that you are not strong enough to tell your partner what you need and want. You may close up and keep those things hidden. You can take this leap. Your partner may not understand in the moment, but long term, *they want to be with someone happy.* Someone who knows how to create their own happiness. Your needs are worth sharing.

Once you determine what you need to be happy, share your list with your mate. Let them share theirs.

Make a commitment to each other to put each other first to help support your mate's list and happiness. Sign a contract with one another and keep those priorities over all other people or commitments. No matter what comes up in life, put your partner first.

With a partner who puts you first, who would ever leave?

Relationships are only strong if they support and fulfill the needs and desires of each individual. It takes courage to talk to your partner and communicate your needs.

It takes courage to set up boundaries around your time and mind to live the life that you love and have been accustomed to. Sometimes you may feel that you are being extravagant by taking time for yourself. This can be especially true for the things that bring you joy but do not bring as much for your partner.

It takes courage to hold your mate to their commitment to support your desires when they have neglected them, but you are worthy of your life.

At the end of the day, you are truly your own best friend.

No one will love you like you.

TRUST GOD TO CHOOSE FOR YOU
God is love.

There is an abundance of love in God.

The lie is that there is a lack of what you need and that you have to go searching for love.

This is not true.

We are all created with a desire for love. If you have that desire within you, it was not put there to be unfulfilled.

You may have blocks that keep you from receiving love. Only you know. One of the biggest blocks is thinking that you will not receive love, that you are left out, that somehow something is missing for you.

Sometimes a person's upbringing or life experiences can create this reality for that person.

However, that lie can be overcome with work and time. A scarcity mentality comes from messages you receive and repeat to yourself that become your truth.

Whatever you believe is true for you.

We are all born perfect, created for love and relationships. However, along the way we accept the lie that we are

Not good enough
Not good-looking enough
Too young
Too fat
Too thin
Not smart enough
Too poor
Too rich
Too old

to receive the love we want so desperately.

You must uncover and reject those messages, accept the truth, and repeat higher truths to your inner self until you believe.

The truth is that there is someone perfectly created for you at every stage and point of life.

You have never been lacking. You never will be.

It is time to believe. Along the way, you will receive guidance, encouragement, and help. There are angels all around. God always loves us and wants the best for us. Our job is to stay connected to God and to choose what we believe.

I had a perfectionism problem. I thought I was not good enough, not perfect enough to be loved. This kept me trapped until I realized that I was blocking love. I began to do daily affirmations of higher truth. Over time, I was able to drop the load of perfectionism and accept myself.

My affirmations looked something like this:

Every day is full of all the resources I need to be happy.
I am beautiful inside and out.
I am a light.
I am full of love.
I am a child of the most high.
I have everything I need.
I am right on time.
There are no mistakes.

I easily receive, rest, and trust.
I am created for love.
At the right time, he will be there.
I will receive all the help and comfort I need in the moment I need it.

Your job is to realize that your creator made you for love and relationship.

If you want it, it's out there for you. You don't have to worry or go searching. Love will come to you. Just be conscious, open, hopeful, expectant, and *awake* every day.

Trust yourself. You can enjoy your life until your one comes. You can trust your heart, mind, gut to lead you. Listen intently. Your "picker" isn't broken. God will help you choose.